Waves of Faith

by The Reverend Doctor Dorothea King-James

Waves of Faith

My Life Experiences Shared With Pastor Emeritus Willie Earl James

XULON PRESS

Xulon Press
2301 Lucien Way #415
Maitland, FL 32751
407.339.4217
www.xulonpress.com

© 2023 by Dorothea King-James

All rights reserved solely by the author. The author guarantees all contents are original and do not infringe upon the legal rights of any other person or work. No part of this book may be reproduced in any form without the permission of the author.

Due to the changing nature of the Internet, if there are any web addresses, links, or URLs included in this manuscript, these may have been altered and may no longer be accessible. The views and opinions shared in this book belong solely to the author and do not necessarily reflect those of the publisher. The publisher therefore disclaims responsibility for the views or opinions expressed within the work.

Unless otherwise indicated, Scripture quotations taken from the New King James Version (NKJV). Copyright © 1982 by Thomas Nelson, Inc. Used by permission. All rights reserved.

Scripture quotations taken from the King James Version (KJV) – public domain.

Scripture quotations taken from the Holy Bible, New International Version (NIV). Copyright © 1973, 1978, 1984, 2011 by Biblica, Inc.™. Used by permission. All rights reserved.

Paperback ISBN-13: 978-1-66288-230-2
Ebook ISBN-13: 978-1-66288-231-9

FOREWORD

Faith is often described as a feeling, usually one of optimism. True faith, simply put, is taking God at His word and throwing all our weight on that promise. This is what Abram did when he was told to leave his home and go to a city whose builder and maker was God. So, Abraham did just that. According to Romans 4, he was fully persuaded that what God had promised was what God would deliver. Moving from his hometown and leaving relatives was just his starting point. Later, he would be told that he would become the father of many nations—only there was a problem: not only was his wife, Sarah, past the point of childbearing, but he was, too. As far as they were concerned, they were both dead. But they took God at His word and kept trying and kept waiting and trying, and trying, and trying, and then—the son of promise, Isaac, was born. They did not waver but kept trusting, as demonstrated by their faith and obedience.

In *Waves of Faith*, the author will provide us with some unique waves of experiences, which are like those of our past biblical role models and our pre-contemporary Abrahams and Sarahs of our day and time. Each one of these challenges of faith will reveal how this devoted husband and wife trusted in Almighty God to consistently anchor them as well as propel them in their journey of sharing life.

It is the author's intense hope, as you read this book, *Waves of Faith*, that it will inspire and motivate you to prioritize what is needed in our collective journey, according to Micah 6:8, "He hath showed thee, O man, what is good; and what doth the Lord require of thee, but to do justly, and to love mercy, and to walk humbly with thy God?"

I have observed the author, Dr. King-James, embrace and exhibit this kind of faith during episodes of struggles—and do you know what she did?

She followed God's instructions and turned to her earthly spiritual leader: Jesus' under-shepherd, Rev. Willie Earl James, her husband and pastor. This, dear reader, may not make sense in today's world, but neither did building an ark for a flood when it had never rained before, and neither did it make sense that God would judge His own Son, Jesus the Christ, for our sins and crush him. But true faith tells another story.

God Bless You,
Melvin Clark

TABLE OF CONTENTS

FOREWORD vii
INTRODUCTION xiii
ACKNOWLEDGMENTS xv

CHAPTER ONE: A Chance Meeting 1
CHAPTER TWO: Parenthood: The Path of Patience 9
CHAPTER THREE: The Challenges God's Grace
    Was Sufficient to Meet 11
CHAPTER FOUR: Wave of Love—Establishing
    Our Family Roots 16
CHAPTER FIVE: Jesus Supplies the Answers to Our Needs 18
CHAPTER SIX: Grace Propels Us through Our Struggles 23
CHAPTER SEVEN: Thriving for the Cause of Christ 25
CHAPTER EIGHT: Anchoring Strength in Your Struggles 26
CHAPTER NINE: We Cried Unto the Lord, the Rock,
    Our Salvation 29
CHAPTER TEN: Through It All, God's Love Sustains Us 31
CHAPTER ELEVEN: Our Journey: Celebrating Our
    Thirty-Fifth Wedding Anniversary 34
CHAPTER TWELVE: Saying Farewell Is Never Easy 37

TRIBUTE FOR PASTOR EMERITUS, REVEREND WILLIE
    EARL JAMES, AND MASTER CHAPLAIN 38

FOND MEMORIES: FAMILY, FRIENDS,
   FAMILY FAITH MEMBERS 40
JAMES MCCAIN ("POOKIE") AND WILLIE EARL JAMES:
   THE YOUNGER YEARS IN THE HOOD................ 49
IN TRIBUTE TO PASTOR WILLIE EARL JAMES........... 53
SUMNER HIGH SCHOOL CLASS OF 1968................ 59
SALUTE TO MY FATHER................................. 60
LAST CONSTRUCTED SERMON: PASTOR EMERITUS
   WILLIE EARL JAMES 38
THIRTY-EIGHTH CHURCH ANNIVERSARY SPEECH.... 65
APPENDIX:... 67
   Appendix Image One: Original Bus Transfer From
      Our Original Meeting 67
   Appendix Image Two: Our Wedding Ceremony................. 68
   Appendix Image Three: First Year of Marriage 68
   Appendix Image Four: Thirty-Seven Reasons For Our Love 69
   Appendix Image Five: We Jumped This Broom On
      Our Wedding Day 69
   Appendix Image Six: Husband & Wife 70
   Appendix Image Seven: Pastor Emeritus Willie Earl James &
      Minister Melvin Clark 70
   Appendix Image Eight: Original Poem –
      Husband to You From Me......................... 71
   Appendix Image Nine: Original Poem- Wife Love is
      a Treasured Keepsake 72
   Appendix Image Ten: New Ebenezer Missionary Baptist Church
      of The Ville- Our Place of Worship for Forty-Three Years ... 73
   Appendix Image Eleven: Pastor Emeritus Willie Earl James
      Bible Study 73

Appendix Image Twelve: Husband's Trophy Fish................ 74
Appendix Image Thirteen: "The Man, The Myth, The Legend..." . 74
Appendix Image Fourteen: Our Thirty-Fifth Wedding
    Celebration With Initial Cakes "W" And "D" 75
Appendix Image Fifteen :- Celebrants Seated at
    Table of Honor 75
Appendix Image Sixteen :- A Kiss To Seal Our Joy 76
Appendix Image Seventeen :-Jointly Holding Knife to
    Cut Our Cakes 76
Appendix Image Eighteen : We are Actually Cutting the Cake ... 77
Appendix Image Nineteen :Wife is Giving Her Husband His
    First Bite of Our Cake 77
Appendix Image Twenty: Husband is Giving His Wife
    Her First Bite of Our Cake 78
Appendix Image Twenty-One: Willie and Dorothea
    are Standing In Front of Our Home 78
Appendix Image Twenty-Two : A Moment of Intimacy 79

ABOUT THE AUTHOR.. 83

INTRODUCTION

Waves of Faith will highlight the mundane issues that each member of the human family must grapple with to successfully anchor you through your temporary life and balance these experiences to reach the proverbial rainbow on the other side of life's struggles. After this balance is achieved, we will embrace our true home of rest and everlasting joy. In this life, we will experience undulant waves of challenges: How one navigates through the waves at each stage will test your life by asking, "What is faith?" "What or who can stabilize us as we confront our waves of faith?"

Faith is the intrinsic belief which does not question or ask for proof about God or religion. For example: Job kept his faith during his trouble. Job was loyal to his belief, and he exercised a strong sense of duty, as a true believer should in time of challenges. Generally, waves move up and down, or back and forth. Waves also can suddenly rise and increase in intensity. One can experience a wave of anger, a wave of joy, or a wave of sadness. Whatever the circumstances of the wave experience, one needs to remain faithful, be dependable, and stay true to that person or thing by the bond which was taken in his or her verbal oath. Striving to become a faithful husband or a faithful wife takes demonstrating to that person your complete loyalty and trust. I desire to share my truth with others who have had to deal with issues in their interactions with others—in their immediate family circles or their extended family members. I have personally experienced that many people do not really value or appreciate your uniqueness of being "you" and "your" own person, nor your willingness to compromise your dignity of who you are. My goal is to leave a living legacy for my nuclear family, their children, and their children's children. Through the words and experiences in my life, I wish to guide them, to navigate them successfully through their waves: storms and short-lived turbulences they will encounter in life. I am writing this book to share my unique experiences as a wife, mother, nurse, sister, auntie, grandmother, great-grandmother, cousin, and friend to those who have not discovered that, regardless of the challenges in this life, with the good, bad, and ugly, you can find meaning, discover value, and leave a cherished life behind.

ACKNOWLEDGMENTS

To the one true God, in the essence of the Trinity: Father, Son, Holy Spirit. Thank you for providing the financial resources, health, and strength. It was You, Father God, who planted this seed of faith in my heart to write this narrative about my shared journey with my beloved husband, Pastor Emeritus Willie Earl James. He was my best friend; we shared our life together for forty-two years, until death separated us.

Our lives were dedicated to Almighty God by sharing in service for all mankind. Our lives as a couple certainly went through our waves of faith, and we faced them all courageously together. Our life's journey has been an intercurrent of interpersonal challenges within our faith, family, and friends. We have endeavored to accept and maintain our focus of growing our faith, expanding our family, and prioritizing our friends while maintaining our relationship with our true and living God, Jehovah. Our biblical ancestry is linked and likened to that of Abram and Sari. We, too, had difficulty starting our family. Although ours didn't take as long as theirs, this was a challenge, and we remained faithful. Abram and Sari finally got their child of promise. Isaac was born. Our eldest daughter was finally born. After the birth of Isaac, Abram's name was changed from Abram to Abraham, and his wife's name from Sari to Sarah. Our acquired names are quite important; my husband obtained his name from his uncle, and mine was obtained from my mother. Each of us, in God's creation, has been predestined to fulfill various roles within our nuclear and extended families. Our spheres of influence solidified as we were joined as husband and wife. Our primary objective was the call of God to make disciples in God's kingdom building. We had to remember that we were called, and that God Jehovah qualified our call into this ministry of reconciliation. God has equipped each of us with a spiritual anchor to withstand the unexpected storms of life, when the billows are tossing us throughout life's seas. We must make sure that we are truly utilizing the anchor of God's Word, which is our Holy Bible. This book contains basic instruction for living a holistic life. Here is an appropriate acronym for this sacred book:

(B)asic (I)nstruction (B)efore (L)eaving (E)arth

It also encourages us by example and commands us to regularly assess our personal and spiritual conditions. Each of us, while on life's journey, will need this sacred roadmap to reach those eternal shores, beyond God's celestial seas.

When we accomplish our specific tasks in this life journey on Earth, we will leave our temporary houses and lands to journey to our eternal home. We will receive our custom-made robes, our crowns, and our prepared mansion, which were designed for us. 2 Corinthians 2:9 says, "But as it is written, eye hath not seen, nor ear heard, neither have entered into the heart of man, the things which God hath prepared for them that love Him."

My heart is certainly grateful for one of my husband's "besties," Minister Melvin Clark. Minister Clark accepted the challenge of writing the Foreword for this book. It's wonderful to know that he can be depended upon in a time of need. God always prepares the hearts of His servant to meet any need in any season.

CHAPTER ONE

A Chance Meeting

On August 8th, I got on a Bi-State bus that was going northbound on Grand Boulevard. I paid my fare and was issued a ticket by the driver, Willie James. I sat near the front so I could view each cross street as the bus proceeded to pick up various passengers at each scheduled stop. I informed the driver that I was on my way downtown to fire my current husband and that he would be receiving his pink discharge slip upon his arrival back home.

This information certainly got the driver's attention. He stated to me, "You don't want to do that. Why don't you let me talk with you about it?"

With that, we exchanged phone numbers and began talking about my decision. I warned him that once I have pondered a decision, it is nearly impossible for me to change my mind. I am a very decisive person. Later that same evening, I did telephone him to discuss my issue.

He shared that he had gone through similar problems, which didn't have good outcomes. Nevertheless, I had made up my mind that this was the best remedy for my unique situation. I was abandoned with two daughters to raise and provide for with no visible means of financial assistance. I had to depend upon public assistance until I could complete my studies at Harris-Stowe College. I persevered through working as a teacher's assistant until I obtained my credentials in education.

I did get my divorce, then I applied for child support, which did not materialize until my daughters were teenagers. The divorce decree was not enforceable because my former ex-husband knew how to play against the system. Anyway, after I got a job at Harris-Stowe, I didn't need to force this issue of receiving child support. I became the family head.

I was employed as a laboratory assistant. I assisted students who were struggling in Biology and other applied sciences. The funds received were just enough to continue paying my rent and my monthly bills. I decided to phone this bus driver, who I had conversed with briefly. He invited me out for pizza. I explained to him that if he indeed wanted to enjoy my company on a scheduled date, my daughters would need to go out with us on this pizza date.

Our first date was at Imo's Pizza, located near Forest Park. We ordered pizza and beverages and had an enjoyable time. After we finished eating our meal, my oldest daughter inquired about taking another one home. I could sense from my date's eyes that his response was, "**No**."

I said, "That's okay; we can eat again when we get back home." I reprimanded my daughter for being rude and greedy. My date later phoned me and said that he did not want to go through that experience again.

So, I began having him come over to my apartment after his preaching engagements, and I did not mind cooking for him. This was the beginning of our courtship period. I lived in the city of St. Louis, and he lived in the county of St. Louis.

After about a year of dating, he proposed to me while I was washing dishes. I was a little reluctant at first, but I accepted his proposal of marriage. Initially, we had planned a March wedding date, but we had an unfortunate setback. Willie was given some medication that he was allergic to, and his skin broke out in a noticeable rash. So, we decided to postpone our plans until later.

Once my fiancé was well, we decided to secure another wedding date. Since we both had monthly expenses, he decided to move me into his apartment. I gave my apartment manager my two weeks' notice of my move-out date. My children transferred from the city school district to the county school district. We gathered our participants for our wedding day. All the groom's participants were preachers, and mine were family members and two friends.

We had our wedding catered by two friends, Roger and Thelma. They made sure everything was cooked and seasoned to perfection. My mother prepared seventy pounds of turnips and mustard greens. They were enjoyed by all who tasted this Southern cuisine. When something is very tasty and delicious, there is a unanimous expression: "She put her big toe in this!"

Thelma and Roger prepared the side dishes for this meal. They cooked fried chicken, macaroni and cheese, yeast rolls, and black-eyed peas. Our wedding guests appeared to be pleased with the meal selection and the excellent caterers. We certainly enjoyed our special day. The celebration concluded with the jumping of the broom. We spent our weekend together, and we purposely woke early the next morning, which was our Christian Sabbath. We went back to the church, where we exchanged our sacred vows. This time, our worship experience was very special, because we were worshipping together as husband and wife: two became one.

Shortly after our marriage, my husband began having some health issues. I promised him that I had taken my wedding vows seriously. "In sickness and in health, for richer or poorer, until death do us part."

Once his health issues were stabilized, we began talking about expanding our family. We got pregnant after two years of marriage, and our two daughters would welcome their sister into the world. Our daughter was born alert and healthy and was breast-fed.

After giving birth to our daughter, I continued to pursue my educational goals. I pumped my breast milk daily and froze it for our babysitter. Our babysitter was a member of our family. She would watch our newborn daughter while we both worked. I had to remain at the babysitter's home until my husband got off work. This made for a very long day for us. However, once home, I would prepare a hot, delicious meal for the family. My husband really enjoyed my cooking. He once invited his auntie and his mother to sample my cooking. It was a large meal with all the trimmings. After we had dined and finished our meal, his auntie said, "I know one thing: you surely got a good cook."

After we had adjusted to our apartment, we decided to look for a house. Basically, we needed more space. We did find one, and it was not far from where we were living. We began packing up to relocate to our new home. My children were excited because they would have more room. My daughters would share one room, and we had our space and more privacy. We had to secure a solid bed for our girls. So, we purchased a wooden bunk bed set. The oldest daughter wanted the lowest bed and the youngest the upper bunk. Our youngest daughter slept wildly; she would occasionally fall out of the bed. In order to keep her safe, we purchased bed railings to secure her safety while sleeping. With this problem solved, we focused on making the rest of the furniture purchases for our home. We needed a kitchen table, a sofa for the living room, a desk for my husband's study, and shelving for our many books we both had acquired through the years. I could sew, so I made curtains for our living room. We decided to keep the hardwood flooring and just utilize small rugs for the entryway to our front door.

We had to register our children for school and purchase the needed supplies for a successful school year. There was a small shopping center within walking distance. We would walk there and pick up a few odds and ends for our home. After getting our home comfortable for a year, we decided to get pregnant, but my husband struggled with health issues, which delayed us from becoming pregnant sooner.

It took a few years, and once we finally got pregnant, my children learned that they would be welcoming a little sister or brother. Our daughters were enrolled in school. Our youngest was in preschool until she was eligible for kindergarten. Our next daughter would continue going to the babysitter. Each evening, I would prepare the children's lunch sacks, complete with their names written on the outsides and love notes stuffed into the insides, all waiting for them in the refrigerator.

My husband would then take me to work, as I did not know how to drive, nor did I have a license to operate a motor vehicle. This was a hurdle that we needed to solve. My husband would patiently take me out on the weekends to teach me how to operate a car. I simply was not ready to drive yet, so he kept driving me day after day, month after month, and year after year. I finally announced to my husband that I was ready to focus on obtaining my license to operate a motor vehicle. My husband was an excellent driving instructor. He would hand me the keys and allow me to drive through our neighborhood. I could drive, but parallel parking was my biggest challenge. Every time I attempted to park, I ended up on the curb. I practiced parking between two trash cans. I would always knock them down. My husband said, "You are not ready yet." Willie would allow me to drive, and he would then park for me. I did not know that "thing of parking the car" would prevent me from securing my driver's license. After about a month, I made an announcement to my husband.

"Willie, I think I am ready to obtain my official driver's license." Unknown to me, my husband had prayed, "Lord, You know that she is not ready to drive safely, so let her fail this road test."

Well, I indeed failed, and how disappointing was this. Another month passed, and I felt ready to secure my license. Because my husband allowed me to drive to the motor vehicle office, I parked and obtained my learner's permit. I could continue practicing my driving while a licensed driver was in the vehicle. I then got two trash cans to practice my parallel parking. I practiced consistently for two weeks. I parked the car without hitting or knocking the trash cans down. I then asked my two daughters to stand in and pretend that they were the trash cans. I got into the car and successfully maneuvered our vehicle between our two daughters. This was certainly done with a wave of faith.

The next day, my husband and I drove to the motor vehicle office, and I successfully obtained my driver's license. I was so elated over this accomplishment that I shouted, "Hallelujah to God Jehovah for making this a reality!" Now that I am a licensed driver, I have the freedom to do other things without being an additional burden to my beloved husband. I can drive alone.

I still had another problem. I really needed to focus on learning street signs and directions. I would sometimes get lost and would have to phone my husband to rescue me. My favorite expression was "beam me home, Scottie." I needed to overcome my dependence on "Scottie" and truly learn to navigate my way safely from point A to point B without an incident or accident. Out of caution, my husband would still occasionally drive me or allow me to take the bus to work. I would then have to arrange transportation back home. We only had one vehicle, and he could not allow me to have an accident in our only means of transportation.

Another challenge surfaced when I received my new job assignment. I was to work at Northwest High School as a resource teacher. This position lasted for one year. The next year, I was reassigned to be the balance to this school's Caucasian staffing. Since I had no building seniority, the unwritten rule was "last staff hired is the first to be transferred to another work site." This was really a major wave of faith, because the location was the extreme southside of the city. This new job assignment and new location was known as Cleveland High School. My husband was not overjoyed about my job site assignment. However, being the man that he was, he knew what was needed to solve this dilemma. Willie would drive me daily to my new job assignment for a month. I could see that this was a physical strain on my husband. I began to ask various staff persons for a ride back home. I befriended a math teacher who was a true blessing to us. She would take me to my front door after we had completed our work duty. I didn't want to wear my welcome out. So, I asked another staff person if she would allow me to ride with her. This was our second simultaneous blessing God Jehovah provided. I was given transportation to work and back home. I was so relieved. Now, my husband could get the physical rest his body needed. My husband worked the second shift, so this was a super blessing for our family. I had the necessary time to prepare our family with a hot, nourishing meal after our daily routines had been fulfilled.

Our children were steadily getting their education. Our routine was working and making a decent living. We finally got pregnant with another child. My baby bump, now visible, caused me to purchase some maternity clothes to add a layer of comfort for my developing baby and me. I shared a classroom with another teacher, with the same teaching specialty, who was very supportive. Our specialty was educating children with specific learning disabilities, behavior disorders, and Educable Mental Retardation. We both were responsible for organizing daily curriculum to support those students who struggled with their individual academic challenges. Our classroom was a diverse one, in that we were educating students from different ethnic backgrounds. The student population was mostly Caucasian and very few students of color. This was the primary reason for transferring me from Northwest High School to Cleveland High School: to balance the instructional staff with educators of color.

After working at Cleveland for two years, I became aware that many children were being socially promoted to the secondary level, basically because of their chronological ages. I felt that this was a disservice for them academically. I strived to correct this problem by requesting a transfer to a middle school to rescue many of these deficient students who had not achieved mastery in their basic reading skills. My new job assignment was Clinton Middle School. I remained there until the school closed due to low enrollment.

After this, I was assigned to Stevens Middle School as a Resource Teacher. This school provided an ideal setting and structure to meet the individualized needs of the students. These students needed their daily curriculum modified to garner academic successes. It was at this school that I got involved with the Drug-Free Schools after-school extracurricular activities. This program provided students with a positive outlet for them to increase their self-worth and avoid negative peer pressure. I developed and organized the Natural High Talent Show. Students could audition during their study hall periods or after school. Many students showcased their talents and performed for the school community. This became our family affair. My husband would video-record each performance, and our children would assist by serving as ushers and seating our special performers and guests from the school community. The staff and students really enjoyed this alternative setting while learning refusal skills to say "Yes" to life and "No" to drugs. We did vignettes, anti-drug rapping, and dancing. We awarded our student performers first-, second-, and third-place prizes for the best group performances. Our entire family really enjoyed assisting me with this extracurricular event. This event occurred every spring. Through this program, a stipend was given for us to hire additional staff to guide these students in choosing to embrace drug-free lifestyles. We purchased plain tee-shirts, and we designed them with catchy anti-drug slogans on them.

The student participants wore their designed tee-shirts and modeled them during the Natural High Talent Show. This show was so very successful locally that our school received a monetary grant and a free performance from Channel 11 Power Teen Club, who were also advocates of promoting drug-free lifestyles. Our school received national recognition for implementing an effective model for Drug-Free Education. We received an award from the Department of Education during the 1993-1994 school year. This was quite an honor for our local school district as we attended the awards ceremony in Washington, DC on June 2 and June 3, 1994.

CHAPTER TWO

Parenthood: The Path to Patience

Parenthood has many unforeseen challenges, which can stretch you beyond your capacity to cope, especially when you are trying your absolute best to meet your children's needs. It would have been an emotional hurricane if we didn't have an anchor of hope to lean on when those challenges surfaced. Our daughters were very focused upon their studies and engaged in the rigor of meeting their curriculum expectations.

However, it wasn't the case with our sons. Our second-oldest son and our youngest gave us enormous emotional waves in their non-adjustments to rules reinforcement. They both failed to report to school on time and also refused to complete and turn in their expected assignments. Our youngest son had to repeat the eighth-grade curriculum twice, before being promoted to high school. Our second-oldest son seemed to be exhibiting non-compliant behaviors in most of his assigned classes.

We didn't know the immediate cause of his disruptive behavior. My husband and I tried to get a remedy for his issues by having him evaluated for Special Education. He was demonstrating all the visual signs of a student with a diagnosis of Behavior Disorder. Our second-oldest son was extremely hostile toward those who were in a position of authority. He refused to complete his assigned learning tasks. Since my professional training was in this specialized area, we decided to utilize my training in behavior modification techniques to aid our son's non-compliant school issues.

We conferenced with our son and explained that he needed to own his inappropriate behaviors and that they needed to change immediately, especially if he wanted to prepare for a successful life. He needed a quality education. He was asked to take a behavior monitoring sheet from our home to school daily. His various assigned teachers were asked to observe and evaluate our second-oldest son's behavior in their classrooms. If our son's behavior was less than satisfactory, he would lose weekend privileges. To our surprise, this behavior monitoring sheet was quite effective, as it provided a critical link from home to school. This really assisted in modifying our son's inappropriate behaviors. We received less phone calls from school. We also gave our son a small notebook to write down how he was dealing with his emotions throughout his school day. He didn't need to be formally evaluated because he was blessed to have a qualified mother at home. When the parent, student, and school, work together to force change in unifying, consistent efforts, we were successful in causing a positive change in our son's attitude toward those in positions of authority. My husband and I were given a pleasant surprise during one of our worship services. Our second-oldest got up and shared his testimony that he, indeed, had experienced a miraculous change.

We solved our youngest son's problem by getting him a car to make it to school on time. He would usually miss his scheduled school bus. This resolved his issues with school.

CHAPTER THREE

The Challenges: God's Grace was Sufficient to Meet Our Needs

My challenge began in the summer of 1980. My husband, the Reverend Willie Earl James, was called to pastor a church while he was dealing with a medical handicap that required him to be placed on a kidney machine three times weekly to sustain his life. These hemodialysis treatments continued for three and a half years from the day his kidney stopped functioning in March of 1980. I had to pay particular attention to his diet; his food had to be weighed, his sodium intake was restricted, and his blood pressure had to be monitored daily.

In midst of this challenge, I was trying to maintain a professional career as a classroom teacher, function as a mother of two with another on the way…and be a nurse and helpmeet to this newly called pastor.

As you can clearly see, I was faced with a situation requiring a choice between family and career: to resign my position as classroom teacher or provide the necessary healthcare for my husband. I had enough sense to know that I couldn't endure this situation alone. So, I allowed God to assist me in these challenges that I faced. I had enough faith in God to the degree that I was willing to allow Him to have first place in this serious decision-making process which had to be made in order to meet the needs of my family. The Lord gave me the answer, and I thank God through Jesus Christ our Lord that I claimed his recorded Word in Philippians 4:13, which states: "I can do all things through Christ which strengthens me." So, with this, I decided that I could be a good teacher, mother, nurse, and helpmeet.

With this determination, I claimed my husband's healing with this scripture found in Isaiah 53:5: "But he was wounded for our transgressions; he was bruised for our iniquities: the chastisement of our peace was upon Him; and with His stripes we are healed." I accepted, once again, the recorded Word of God: Romans 8:28, "And we know that all things work together for good to them that love God, to them who are the called according to His purpose."

> Romans 8:26 says, "Likewise, the Spirit also helps in our weaknesses. For we do not know what we should pray for as we ought, but the Spirit Himself makes intercession for us with groanings which cannot be uttered."

At this point, my spiritual challenges were beginning to be fulfilled, and I repeated Romans 8:38 for encouragement. "For I am persuaded that neither death nor life, nor angels nor principalities nor power, nor things present nor things to come, nor height nor depth, nor any other created thing, shall be able to separate us from the love of God which is in Christ Jesus our Lord."

Approximately forty years have passed since the day when my husband and I received a telephone call from Veterans Hospital. The caller informed my husband of his gift from heaven… a perfect kidney, which was a perfect tissue match, ready to be transplanted! I knew within my heart that God was about to work His miracle through this team of doctors, by relieving my husband of his medical handicap. After a four-hour operational procedure, my husband and I praised God for His miracle-working power because his operation had been successful. Now, this man of God has more physical energy to do the work that he had been called to do. He could now eat what he wanted to eat and go where he wanted to go. Yet, before this moment, I had to face other waves of faith, while my husband was still in the hospital and the work of the church needed to continue.

I quickly learned the responsibilities the New Ebenezer Missionary Baptist Church congregation wanted me to assume. They expected me to be a jack of all trades and a master of none. In essence, I was the Sunday school superintendent when the superintendent was absent, announcing clerk if she should be absent, and devotional leader if the deacons were absent. Overwhelmed by this, I had to push my panic button and take a righteous stand. I wrote the congregation an open letter expressing my personal aspirations and my expectations before there was a literal explosion! I uttered in my spirit, "Lord Jesus, have mercy on them, for they know not what they are doing," as some of the members decided that this was "Doom's Day for Dorothea" because I was young and inexperienced. Yet, their "Doom's Day" plan backfired because I had petitioned the Lord through prayer for a positive response. I didn't fight this battle in the flesh because I knew and believed these words recorded in Hebrews 4:16: "Let us therefore come boldly unto the throne of grace, that we may obtain mercy, in time of need." I can truly say that all my help comes directly from the Lord, and these are but a few of my experiences of being a pastor helpmeet. Yet, through them all, I have always been encouraged by the words of this song co-authored by F.I. Eiland and Emmett Dean:

"Lord, I want to live for thee, every day and hour,
Let Thy Spirit be with me, In its saving power!
In my weakness be my strength; In my trials all,
Be thou near me all the day, Hear my every call!
Leave me not to walk alone, Lest I droop and die;
Let Thy Spirit go with me; attend my every cry!
Keep my heart and keep my hand,
Keep my soul, I pray
Keep my tongue to speak Thy praise,
Keep me all the way!"

Shortly after receiving our gift from heaven, my husband's employer, Bi-State, decided to downsize their support staff. Through this transitional period, bills began to accumulate. My husband's immediate supervisor arranged his work so he could continue to follow up with his doctors and have his medication adjusted as needed. My husband's immediate supervisor was changed later, and his replacement wasn't as sympathetic to the needs of my husband. My husband overheard his new supervisor talking of eliminating the data clerk position, which would affect my husband's rice bowl. Knowing this, he asked his supervisor a direct question regarding his continued employment with Bi-State. His new supervisor was rather evasive in his response, saying, "Things have a way of slipping out." I am so grateful that things did slip out, because my husband was about to lose his job as well as his benefits. The Lord touched the heart of another supervisor with Bi-State in that she literally created a position to keep my husband on the payroll, and his benefits could continue. I know, without a doubt, that Jesus supplied the answer to our needs.

Once my husband's health was stabilizing, the Lord provided me with an opportunity to obtain my master's degree in education. This was another wave of faith which the Lord brought us through. I graduated in August of 1988. During this trial, it wasn't easy to manage the educational demands of school, family, and job. I named and claimed my desired end. In the midst of this educational process, I persevered through college instructors who had embraced ideologies that were different from mine. After I weathered this storm, I focused my energy on having our fifth child. My husband and I had made an oral agreement that once I obtained my master's degree, we would work on getting pregnant. Well, our fifth-born child was welcomed into the world the next year. The Lord blessed us with a bouncing baby boy. We decided to give him the name of Caleb Emile James. This child reached all the expected milestones without incident. At the time of our son's birth, my first-born child was about to graduate from McCluer North High School. We supported her choice of selecting a Historically Black College, and she made a rather smooth transition from high school to college life. Our second-born child, however, soon after decided to make an early exodus from our parental authority. When she left, I purposely purchased a suitable card to visualize her departure. I released her into the capable hands of the Lord. She had reached the majority age and desired to venture out on her own. I bid her Godspeed and went on with my life. We must realize in every situation we must let go and let God.

CHAPTER FOUR

Wave of Love—
Establishing Our Family Roots

A family must be united by love based upon this scriptural reference:

> If I speak human or angelic tongues but do not have love, I am a noisy gong or a clanging cymbal. If I have the gift of prophecy and understand all mysteries and all knowledge, and if I have all faith so that I can move mountains but do not have love, I am nothing. And if I give away all my possessions, and if I give over my body in order to boast but do not have love, I gain nothing. Love is patient, love is kind. Love does not envy, is not boastful, is not arrogant, is not rude, is not self-seeking, is not irritable, and does not keep a record of wrongs. Love finds no joy in unrighteousness but rejoices in truth. It bears all things, believes all things, hopes all things, endures all things. (1 Corinthians 13:1–13)

God is Sovereign. God is the ultimate sustainer and promise keeper. God supplies His blessings on those who are obedient; especially to those who walk upright in His Word. God's people will receive punishment for their disobedience.

God's pure love for His creation includes immediate correction for our willfull disobedience. For example: our fore parents Adam and Eve, were evicted from the Garden of Eden; because they both willfully disobeyed

God's command. AlmightyGod desires our obedience. Absolutely no problem is too big to stop a plan made in the will of God. " For I know the plans I have for you," this is the Lord's declaration, "plans for your well-being, not for disaster, to give you a future and a hope. You will call to me and come and pray to me, and I will listen to you. You will seek me and find me when you search for me with your heart." (Jeremiah 29:11).

Our plans should be worthy of God's eye as well as our own. Yesterday's sorrows can be our future successes of today. Hallelujah to our Lord and Savior, Jesus Christ. My husband was convicted by the Holy Spirit to leave behind all things, people, associates, and affiliations that hindered his development in becoming a man after God's own heart. Once God began to prioritize his walk and his life, Willie truly became a vessel of honor to be used entirely by God. My husband thought that he was living the "high life" until God humbled him with the conviction of the Holy Spirit to begin anew in his relationships with the true, divine, living Father of all mankind.

With this fresh revelation, Willie Earl James was blessed with a God-fearing wife for forty-two years. I know, now, that it wasn't a chance meeting of me boarding his bus on Grand; but it paved the path for re-direction of our priorities, our future life, of rebuilding our blended family. We collectively sought those things which would become blessings and not curses. We desired to please God Almighty.

God's stamp of approval has directed our journey through this relationship with Him. True love is being there for someone, through thick and thin. Sharing the same value of oneness with our Creator God. Developing a deeper understanding of intense intimacy with your beloved spouse. This sacred union produced compassionate, God-fearing children. We are truly grateful to God Jehovah for making our lives and lifestyles blend and thrive for forty-two years.

CHAPTER FIVE

Jesus Supplies the Answers to Our Needs

Another wave of faith abruptly entered when my oldest child was involved in a car accident while she and her husband were traveling from Chicago to Saint Louis in the winter. When the accident occurred, they were approximately seventy-two miles outside of Saint Louis, near Litchfield, Illinois. Our daughter, who was in the spring of her life, was pregnant with her first child.

As the accident caused their car to be inoperable, my husband and I utilized personal leave days to come to our daughter's rescue. I thank God and praise God because He provided protection for our child; her husband and her unborn child were not seriously injured. My husband and I brought my daughter and son-in-law back to our home for a temporary visit. Since I realized that this was a traumatic event, I began to minister to them. I decided to write an open letter that was dated January 5, 1996. The letter stated:

> I realize that this unforeseen accident has occurred, but you two must go forward and stop mentally tormenting yourselves. I know interpersonal conflicts have already surfaced! What occurred on Tuesday, January 2, 1996, was an unforeseen event. Before you left Chicago, I prayed and asked the Lord Almighty to keep you and your wife safe from physical harm. God surely answered this prayer.

The Lord smiled on us with two snow days, which enabled me and my husband to come to your rescue!

Now, with that said, Daughter and Son, please, for the sake of your unborn child and my grandchild, try to decrease the emotional tension which the accident created. I have observed it, so please try to release the tension. I pray that you two will seek God's guidance and enter a peaceful agreement today. Remember my motto for living: "I've got a feeling everything's going to be alright!"

Signed: Daughter
Signed: Son- in- Law
Love, Mother and Mother-in-Law

Joyous times sprang forward with the birth of our firstborn's child. My firstborn grandchild was given life on my deceased mother's birthday. I thank and praise God because everything turned out alright. I am truly grateful to God that my children reconciled their differences and recommitted themselves to each other in their marriage. To date, they have celebrated twenty-seven years of matrimony. Now, new challenges began to surface through our third-oldest child, who decided, after high school graduation, to accept a scholarship to a predominantly Jesuit school. Her transitional period within the first year had its ups and downs. However, during the second year, her world was turned literally upside-down. Our daughter suffered, on more than one occasion, from intimidating behavior from her roommate and neighbors who resided in Monroe Hall. She began the year living in Monroe Hall on the second floor, which was designated as a "non-smoking" floor. She had asked for a "non-smoking floor" due to her asthma, which can be triggered by smoke. My daughter registered numerous complaints against her roommates to her residence advisor concerning the smoking of marijuana and tobacco around her room on the second floor of Monroe Hall. Our daughter did not obtain any relief from the resident advisor or the resident director. In fact, her roommate retaliated against our child in response to her pleas for rule enforcement. Our daughter had profanity directed at her and endured her neighbors banging on her dorm room's door and wall all throughout the night. The secondhand smoke gave her difficulty in breathing, persistent coughs, sore throat pain, and recurrent sinus headaches, causing her to miss a significant number of her scheduled classes. These acts of intimidation were so severe that my daughter was unable to bring herself to utilize the bathroom facilities in fear of her own safety. Appalled by these circumstances, my husband and I sought legal advice to address these issues with the school. Our attorney drafted a magnificent letter to support my daughter's allegations that got a quick and favorable response. In the end, however, we decided that our daughter should transfer to another college or university to begin anew and provide an opportunity for her emotional healing. After enrolling at UMSL, she began to seek a degree in foreign language. With the Lord's divine intervention, our daughter received her degree in French in the year 2000. Before her graduation, she obtained an internship at a local translation agency, and, soon after graduating, the Lord blessed her with her first full-time job. It was at a local shoe company that did business internationally.

After working full time for a year and a half, our daughter was surprised by a medical setback. Our daughter suffered a nervous meltdown,, which required psychiatric intervention. Given the diagnosis of bipolar disorder after an event that occurred at church, we were stunned that our daughter had this ailment. She was hospitalized only briefly because she was in total denial of her mental illness. She complied with the doctor's suggestions, only to get discharged from the hospital. Two years after her release, she had to be readmitted because of a medical relapse due to a stressful breakup with a male friend. I counseled our daughter and gave her some sound motherly advice. We both prayed and asked, once again, for a spiritual breakthrough for her mental healing. The Lord Almighty didn't leave or forsake us in our time of need. God always shows up and shows out.

During her hospital stay, as we were celebrating the birthday of our Lord and Savior Jesus Christ, the James household was somewhat bleak. Yet, the Lord gave us strength to go through it. I keep the visual visitor's pass in my vehicle as a reminder of how the Lord blessed us as a family to help our child through her mental nightmare. After this, medical bills began to accumulate for her admission to the hospital. We again petitioned God through prayer and asked for an urgent financial blessing. Through God's divine intervention, we received a response to prayer. The hospital sent a letter stating that they would cancel our daughter's $7,000.00 medical charge. We are so grateful because our daughter had no viable means of repayment.

The Lord surely made a way out of no way. Because of this experience, the words found in Psalm 37:25 have newfound meaning to me: "If you continue to remain steadfast in the Word of the Lord, He will bring all things to pass." Blessed be the name of God, my healer and provider.

It is important to give your all to Jesus because when life's trials and challenges come to test your capacity to withstand the eventful stresses and distresses, you need an anchor to see you safely through. I know that Jesus lives because He has always been by our sides in our times of need. Although there have been many challenges that have tested our family's spiritual foundation, God has been faithful and just to bring us through them all. After going through these trials, I was moved by the Holy Spirit to write God a letter. Within the contents of this letter, I endeavored to thank and praise Him for everything He has blessed me with throughout my brief life of seventy years. In the letter, I said:

Dear God:

I write this letter as a token of my esteem for you as we celebrate the life of your darling Son, Jesus. I am…so very grateful that you allowed your begotten Son who was conceived by the Holy Spirit to come from the womb of a virgin named Mary.

I thank you, holy and righteous Father, for providing the gift of love to the world. You allowed your Son, Jesus, to bridge the gap that separated us from You. It is my desire to develop a closer relationship with You. It is my goal to continue to preach and share the truth of Your Word with others. For I know this is the foundation of my spiritual growth. Thank you for every opportunity that You have blessed me to share the words stated in 2 Timothy 2:13. I ask for Your continued mercy where I have fallen short of implementing all the tasks that should have been completed. I am still striving to continue to walk in Your Word. I ask that you allow Your peace to be planted and cultivated in each born-again believer's heart and mind. As I reflect upon the tasks that You ordained for my hands to do, I stand in awe of Your wisdom. Father God, as we make ready to celebrate the One who sacrificed much, I offer these sincere words of gratitude. Please continue, dear Father, to lead and guide me deeper into Your Word.

Your faithful servant-leader,
Reverend Dr. Dorothea Louise King-James

CHAPTER SIX

Grace Propels Us Through Our Struggles

My husband's creatine levels were beginning to increase at an alarming rate. His practicing nephrologist didn't want him to get any sicker. It was recommended that my husband restart his hemodialysis treatments. Basically, the donor kidney, which was received in 1981, wasn't adequately removing all the harmful toxins from his blood.

We prayed after receiving this pronouncement from his treating physician on May 20, 2015. We visited the Fresenius Dialysis Treatment Center on Thursday, May 28, 2015. My husband's first treatment was June 3, 2015.

This machine was very strange to look at, but it had all the necessary technical parts to perform what a non-working, natural kidney could not do. I watched as my husband's blood was being filtered through this blood pump and the dialyzer. When the blood had been circulated and cleaned through this hemodialysis process, it was returned to his body. This process was necessary to sustain my husband's life a little longer.

My husband was such a champion; he accepted these necessary treatments as his additional work assignments. Willie often would announce to us, "I got to go to work, and I'll see you later." His cycle of work was scheduled three times weekly on Monday, Tuesday, and Friday. The duration of each treatment was four continuous hours. I would often drive him and wait until he finished this process. We also had to go every three months to have his medical access checked to make sure there wasn't any blockage. He faithfully received all his scheduled treatments from 2015 until 2021.

I am grateful that my husband's life was extended so he could complete the tasks that he was called to perform. My husband was very passionate about community policing. He actually desired to be a police officer. Even though this passion never materialized, he did serve as a police chaplain for the city and county for thirty-five years. He also had credentials as a master chaplain. We were blessed to go to Jamacia for this formal ceremony. My husband was so very proud to receive this honor, and I was too. Being a man who bore his cross daily and responded to all who needed his services, a true servant leader, a man after God's own heart, Willie exhibited a tenacious spirit in his daily life. He received each physical challenge and setback with renewed vigor and resolve.

CHAPTER SEVEN

Thriving For The Cause of Christ

My husband, Willie Earl James, served victims of homicides for twelve years, as did I. We have ministered to innumerable families impacted by insensitive acts of gun violence. We assisted them through the crises and supported their families during their funeral services. Prior to COVID-19, we would faithfully attend the funerals, read our formal letters of condolence, and remain through the conclusions of the services. The families were given our contact information, and we offered prayer, counseling, and other resources to assist the grieving families. There was usually a major void of income to funeralize their loved ones who had left this life violently, so GoFundMe pages would offset the burial expenses.

    The families of victims of crime can receive reimbursement of $5,000.00 through the state. The only stipulation is that the funeral costs must be documented via paid receipts. Then, they are compensated for their loved ones' funeral expenses as well as lost wages or salaries from their jobs. This is a beautiful way to strive to make the victims' families whole during the initial recoveries after the tragedies. Community resources are also available through the Missouri Crime Victim Center. They offer one-on-one counseling for victims experiencing such tragic losses.

CHAPTER EIGHT

"Anchoring Strength in Your Struggles"

*Note: These words were shared virtually by Pastor Emeritus Willie Earl James on April 25, 2021.

This day, we are meeting at a point that is shared by most, if not all, of us. A point that is uncomfortable and causes us to recall the pain and anger we so often feel. A point that wants to paralyze us and tries its best to hold us in that state and locks us in our pain and emotions as we mourn the loss of our loved ones. This is the reality of evil that is right in our faces as we strive to cope, to gain a new "normal." We are here today because so many of our loved ones were taken from us through a senseless act by someone who had no respect for human life. Our loved ones were victims of a society that has lost its awareness of how precious life truly is. Although we embrace this point of hurt and pain, it's up to us to decide if we will remain where we are. I challenge you to encourage others, to rise above this reality of fear and become a catalyst of change.

> "For God has not given us the spirit of fear, but of power, and of love and a sound mind" (2 Timothy 1:7).

We are met with defeat if we allow ourselves to live and be comfortable in a hostile society[…]. For many of us, these past months have been the most difficult time of our lives. For others, it has been a constant series of one thing after another. If you have not been there yet, just keep on living, because life has a way of causing us some uncomfortable situations. In Isaiah 40:27–31, the man of God teaches some of the great truths about God—truths that would bring healing to the wounded souls of those who would endure their distresses and sorrows. I believe this passage is full of practical truths that faithful people of God can depend upon under any circumstances of loss or grief. The text reminds us of three fundamental things about God with which we deal.

God is aware when something bad happens to someone.

When we are in our crises of life, we must remember who God is, and allow what we know about Him to help us through our present situations.

God is aware of what His people are facing.

The prophet Isaiah points out some characteristics of God which makes God who He is: omniscient—he know all things, at all times. You can never tell God anything about Himself that He doesn't know. The Lord is everlasting. He has always been and will always be. God is Creator and Sustainer of the Universe. God is able; nothing is impossible with God. He has the power to do what He wants. God is omnipotent, no matter the circumstance or situation you face. There is nothing beyond His ability.

God is available. He is available for those who wait on Him. This availability was supremely manifested by the Savior. He said, in Matthew 11:28, "Come unto me all who labor and are heavy laden, and I will give you rest." In Isaiah 40:28, A question was asked, and a statement was made. It let the Israelites know that God doesn't ever sleep and, at all times, knows what's going on around Him. There is no searching of His understanding. You cannot figure God out. Isaiah says in verse 30, "Even the youths shall faint and be weary, and the young men shall utterly fall." Youths are in the springtime of their lives, physically. Their bodies are strong; they would, in the day of Israel, be the ones who could run. Isaiah not only mentions youths, but he also mentions young men. These are those who are slightly older and are symbols of strength and vigor. The prophet Isaiah says these young men shall utterly fall. Their energy is not endless, which shows us man at his strongest is weak. We stumble, but we don't fall completely, because God's hand is always there to catch us. Sometimes, life is so difficult that we, too, feel like those in this text, that God is not with us, nor does He see the needs we have. Then comes this wonderful message in our text.

Those who look to the Lord will have their strength renewed. He is the one we should look to. When we recognize our weaknesses, He will give us the strength to overcome them. When you realize just how bad things are, look to the Lord for renewed strength. He gives us strength, then, to mount up with wings, as an eagle. Think about this: with little effort, an eagle soars high into the sky, and then, for hours on end, that same eagle can glide far above the earth. This eagle is a symbol of strength and power. The lesson here is that God will strengthen us so that, in our running and walking, we will not grow weary. That's not saying that God's people never grow weary. All of us experience weaknesses. Some experience weakness to a greater degree than others, through all the pressures of life. Sometimes, we wonder if we can go on. Just who are the recipients of this renewed strength? They who wait upon the Lord shall renew their strength. To "wait" means to expect that the Lord will send the strength we need. For He alone is our strength. Be encouraged my brother; be encouraged, my sister. God knows your situations perfectly, and He can do something about it. You cannot hurry Him; you just have to wait. God alone has the capacity, the power, and the resources to meet all the challenges of life, whether they pertain to spirit, body, or soul. God will provide you the anchoring strength during your struggles.

CHAPTER NINE

We Cried Unto The Lord, The Rock of Our Salvation

This is the narrative of my husband's cancer journey. My husband's left fistula graft needed to be removed and then placed into his right artery. Prior to this surgical procedure, he had to complete a treadmill echo test. He obtained his surgical procedure at the Mercy South Hospital. After this surgery, he had to follow up with his heart specialist at the Mercy Clinic Heart and Vascular Hospital.

This surgery was successful. My husband later developed hypoglycemia; he displayed all the observable symptoms of this disorder. He had physical shakiness, rapid heartbeat, sweating, nervousness, dizziness, headache, weakness, and irritability. Once again, we had to check his blood sugar daily to determine if it was low. He was given four ounces of apple or grape juice if it needed a boost. After this treatment, we would have to retest his blood again. A blood sugar level less than 70 mg is considered low. To be prepared for these occurrences, he would have to eat and keep hard candy on hand.

After getting through this hurdle, my husband had a surgical procedure to deal with a growth that was about the size of a small orange. This surgery was performed at Christian Hospital, and it was successful. This growth was removed and examined. This mass disclosed that my husband had lymphoma, which is a blood cancer. A cancer specialist expressed an urgent need for chemotherapy.

My husband and I cried when this initial diagnosis was pronounced. Later, after prayer and meditation, we decided to go ahead with this treatment plan. We continued this recommended therapy for about two painful months. However, my husband started having adverse physical symptoms, which he could no longer tolerate. We decided to discontinue them and lean and depend on Jehovah-Rapha, our healer. The specialist who recommended this therapy was very direct with us. She pronounced to my husband and me that the kind of cancer which my husband had was rapid, and that I should go home and prepare for his funeral. This pronouncement was given in the spring of 2016.

We decided not to schedule any more chemotherapy and just trust God for my husband's total physical and emotional healing. This was a very traumatic event in our lives, and we changed his nephrologist, because this growth which my husband had was the result of pure negligence on his doctor's watch. This doctor had advised my husband not to bother this growth if it wasn't bothering him. If we had continued to follow this doctor's advice, perhaps my husband would have died even sooner.

Through it all, we further depended on our Lord and Savior, Jesus Christ. My husband's surgery was successful, and we worshipped and praised Almighty God for his deliverance.

CHAPTER TEN

Through It All, God's Love Sustains Us

We are grateful to God because Jehovah God has sustained us through all the various health challenges my husband and I endured. Because of our commitment to our wedding vows, "in sickness and in health," we decided to be more purposeful in demonstrating our love to each other. Before our bedside ritual, we would both kneel and openly express, through prayers, our gratitude to Jehovah-Jireh for giving us renewed strength to persevere through the current emotional and physical struggles.

My husband would sometimes woo me through the reading of passages from the Song of Solomon 4:1–7:

> Behold, thou art fair, my love! Behold, thou art fair! Thou hast dove eyes within thy locks. Thy hair is as a flock of goats that appear from Mount Gilead. Thy teeth are like a flock of sheep that are even shorn, which came up from washing whereof everyone bear twins, and none is barren among them. Thy lips are like a thread of scarlet, and thy speech is comely: thy temples are like a piece of a pomegranate within thy locks. Thy neck is like the tower of David built for an armory whereon there hang a thousand bucklers, all shields of mighty men. Thy two breasts are like two young roes that are twins, which feed among the lilies. Until the daybreak, and the shadows flee away, I will get me to the mountain of myrrh, and

to the hill of frankincense. Thou art all fair, my love; there is no spot in thee.

These Scripture verses highlighted our mutual love we had for one another.

My husband wrote this very touching poem for me on Valentine's Day:

For You from Me
by Reverend Willie Earl James

I crave your honesty on the day of love,
Love you wholeheartedly, my sweet dove,
Out of the blue you shout from the sky,
Vividly, beautifully, stunning my eye
Ever adoring you is what I do best.
Your smile, your face, and all the rest.
On days like these I truly believe
You and I are meant to be.

I also wrote a poem to my beloved:
Love is a Treasured Keepsake
Love is a treasured keepsake
You never want to lose it
When you discover this treasure, you'll
Always strive to caress it and hold it
Deep within your arms!
This treasure makes you smile in the midst of your finite pain,
It will evoke laughter when your body is strained,
Love is a treasured keepsake,
You never want to abuse it,
Because this treasure is far too precious to lose it.

Through our journey with life and raising our children to become success stories, we had to face the reality that comes with raising God-fearing children. A family needs order to function properly; it must have unity and love shown toward each other. God places His highest value on love and unity within the family. When families come together with a loving spirit and unity, it's a beautiful thing. These are the truths about realistic parenting. Parenting is hard work; it is expensive and exhausting. It takes a lot of patience, time, love, and dedication to raise children.

Being a mother is a title worthy of much respect and adoration. A mother must be emotionally balanced as she strives to view her children as individuals and help them achieve their own independence. A mother must be committed to motherhood, regardless of other responsibilities outside the home. A realistic mother realizes that her children must be her top priority. My husband was an ideal father, as he accepted his position as the dominant role model in our nuclear family. He was the head of our family and the chief breadwinner. He knew that his sole responsibility was to care for, protect, and provide for his family's needs. Being an ideal father wasn't difficult for my husband, because he didn't have an identity problem. He knew the difference between a daddy and a father. My husband was a man in every sense of that word. He was a real man who stood firm on a decision, whether it was right or wrongt. He was willing to be responsible and accepted his responsibilities. He was a man who knew how to forgive. My husband was a real man who knew how to give respect i to gain respect. My husband knew his place and led his children by his example. He was a God-fearing man who taught those in his family that a praying man is one who leads his family in prayer. When one wears the title of an ideal father, one just can't conclude without talking about God. My husband knew that God was the head of his life. Like David, my husband can say, "The Lord is my shepherd. I shall not want." My husband trusted and knew that God will and can provide whatever one needs. Since God instituted the family, it will strive and be all that it is designed to be when love, nurturing, and support is exhibited within the family circle.

CHAPTER ELEVEN

Our Journey: Celebrating Our Thirty-fifth Wedding Anniversary

We gathered and celebrated our wedding anniversary. We hoped that this special day that means so much would be blessed by the Lord with His loving touch.

We have had some joyful, painful, delightful, laughable, grateful times, because we have experienced them together. It was a most joyful experience for us when our two hearts were united in holy matrimony. Life is, indeed, a mixture of sunshine and rain…because a short time after the sunny times, sad moments entered when we had to accept your many health challenges, which I am thankful to God for seeing us through them; it was painful to observe all the physical pain you had to endure during your ill health, but we remained faithful and trusted God, because we believed "With His stripes, we are healed" Isaiah 53:5.

Delightful moments entered when we acted on God's Word, which states, "Whatsoever you ask in my name, that I will do." Because you then received your "Gift of Life," which was really a gift from heaven because the Lord healed your body. Moments of laughter entered because through the passing days, weeks, months, we didn't forget to laugh during the joyful, delightful, painful, grateful times we shared. We certainly practiced the "L" theory because we lived, laughed, and loved. I am truly grateful to God for allowing a person like me to be your "helpmeet." I would like to thank you for caring and for sharing my successes as well as my disappointments. I am thankful and grateful to God for my family and for our relationship with our Lord and Savior, Jesus Christ.

Our thirty-seventh wedding anniversary was observed with our youngest daughter, Mrs. Trinita Hobbs; her children, Skylar and Harper; and our third-oldest daughter, Lovable Leah James, who had a sentimental surprise awaiting us as we celebrated our thirty-seventh wedding anniversary informally, at home. We were given the task of writing personal sentiments on sticky notes, reading them aloud, and then placing them in a shallow, striped box with a gold-painted #37 in the background. These are some of the sentiments which were posted:

Willie: "We have loved, laughed, cried, and suffered our physical and financial pains. Look at us now (wow). Look at what happens when the right two hearts are joined together with the same goals in mind. (Look at us, girl.)"

Dorothea: "I am pleased to celebrate this day with you, being my very "best friend" to talk out my heart's concerns with."

Willie: "Who would take a well man, when she met him, then he became a sick man, marry him, and nurse him back to health, but you?"

Dorothea: "We have expressed our sacred love through the many sacrifices we have given to preserve this marital relationship."

Willie: "After a failed marriage, I have learned from experience (now) what true marriage is because Dorothea is now my wife for the rest of my life, now, then, and in the life to come. Thank you for loving me the way you do."

Dorothea: "I love you dearly because you have allowed me to be true to myself."

Willie: "After meeting Dorothea for the first time, I had no idea she would be my future wife for many years to come. Life has its way of slowly revealing things to you such as marriage, your children, grandchildren, our home, and in-laws, all because Dorothea and Willie said, 'I do.' Just look at us now, compared to where we both were thirty-six years ago. I was hurting inside, trying to cover up with a smile. Vowing never to be hurt again. Until you came along out of nowhere and brought happiness into my life again."

Dorothea: "Together—the most beautiful word in the language of love."

Our thirty-seven-year marriage has endured the test of time because we faced those challenges together.

CHAPTER TWELVE

Saying Farewell is Never Easy

My husband never meets a stranger; it seems that everywhere we would travel, he always would say, "Hello," and express how good it felt being retired from secular employment. Even though he had retired from working, he still had a calling on his life to preach God's Word, and Pastor Emeritus Willie Earl James endeavored to preach God's Word for thirty-eight years. After his retirement, the last sermon he constructed was entitled "It's All Good." It will be included in the appendix of this book. My husband was called from Earth to glory on Wednesday, September 29, 2021. I was summoned to his hospital bedside and was there when he breathed his last breath. I held his hand and read aloud his favorite Scripture verse: Psalms 24 1–10, "The King of Glory":

The earth is the Lord's and the fullness thereof; the world, and they that dwell therein. For He hath founded it upon the seas, and established it upon the floods. Who shall ascend into the hill of the Lord? Or who shall stand in His holy place? He that has clean hands and a pure heart, who hath not lifted his soul unto vanity, nor sworn deceitfully. He shall receive the blessing from the Lord and righteousness from the God of his salvation. This is the generation of them that seek thy face, O Jacob. Lift up your heads, O ye gates, and be ye lifted up, ye everlasting doors; and the King of Glory shall come in. Who is this King of Glory? The Lord strong and mighty, the Lord mighty in battle. Lift up your heads, O ye gates; even lift them up, ye everlasting doors; and the King of Glory shall come in. Who is this King of Glory? The Lord of hosts, He is the King of Glory.

Tribute for Pastor Emeritus, Reverend Willie Earl James, and Master Chaplain

We honor God because He is God, and to worship God is the highest and holiest of all activities that any human being could ever engage in because it can elevate you from the depths of despair unto the heights of glory! A question was asked of Brother Job. Are you ready for the question? (Yes, we are!)

"If a man die, shall he live again? All the days of my appointed time, I will wait till my change come" Job 14:14.

My beloved husband received his change the other day.

Reverend Willie Earl James was an ordained preacher of God's holy, righteous, and divine Word. My husband burned that midnight oil and drafted numerous sermons. However, there were three that were noteworthy: "An Eagle Stirs the Nest," God's Plum Line," and "Death in the Pot."

My husband was celebrated in 2016 as he retired from city chaplaincy and was dubbed as The Man, The Myth, and The Legend. The Man was a special greeter and guide to First Lady Hillary Clinton. The Myth was cited as Minister of the Year in 1994. The Man served as Bi-State Chaplain and Bi-State Coordinator. The Man also served as a proud chaplain for the City of Saint Louis and Saint Louis County, for a combined total of thirty-five years. The Legend was a tenacious member of the June 14, 1968 Sumner High School. (Are there any Bulldogs in the house?)

The Legend unselfishly gave of his time as well as his talents for the advancement of God's kingdom building. Almighty God certainly equipped me to serve with the Legend as a devoted wife, bedside nurse, lover, coach, and confidante for forty-two years. The young man accepted Christ as Lord and Savior at the tender age of eight, and he was ordained at thirty years of age. He grew and he waxed strong—proclaiming the Gospel Truth to God's Creation! One Lord! One faith! One baptism!

"If a man die, shall he live again?" That question was asked in my introduction.

If a Man, Myth, and Legend dies, will he, the Man, live again? Certainly, the Man will live again because my husband got his spiritual business fix with the giver and sustainer of all life… a long, long time ago.

God is Our Encouragement

Sometimes we feel uncertain
And unsure of everything,
Afraid to make decisions,
Dreading what the day will bring—
We keep wishing it were possible
To dispel all fear and doubt
And to understand more readily
Just what life is all about
God has given us the answers
Which too often go unheeded,
But if we search his promises,
We'll find everything that's needed
To lift our faltering spirits
And renew our courage, too,
For there's absolutely nothing
Too much For God to Do—
For the Lord is our Salvation
And our strength in every fight,
Our Redeemer and Protector,
Our eternal Guiding Light,
Farewell, my Warrior Husband.
"I will see you in the morning, my dear!"

Fond Memories: Family, Friends, Family Faith Members

Fond memories of his children…

Shantana Stewart

Shantana Stewart appreciated Dad for checking up on her to see if she and her family were doing okay.

Ebun Osaze

"One of my fondest memories of Dad, also known as Reverend Willie Earl James, was that he was very supportive of my interest in healthcare. Dad would take me to dialysis with him quite frequently, and I also remember going to the hospital service and initially being placed in the waiting room and told to sit and watch cartoons. One day, Dad spoke up for me and said, "Let her come back and watch," and so, I was super-excited. I didn't really want to watch cartoons, but I was very curious as a child and asked a lot of questions. I was watching them prep Dad, then other patients, for dialysis. I watched the entire process: the mechanics, the procedures, the instrumentation…I believe this really increased my interest in healthcare.

"How I was received and just being fascinated by everything that was going on and watching how he responded and how he interacted taught me great people skills from the point of a patient as well as of a healthcare provider.

"When it was time to resume his dialysis treatments, he knew it was a call to action and something that he could absolutely do with the support of his wife, my amazing mother, who was his best companion and health partner in his journey.

"Today, I am always sharing their journey to inspire and never give up the faith and opportunity to overcome health obstacles. God always has a plan. Hang in there to find out what it is for you!"

Montel D. Harris

"My fond moments with my dad were visits to Lost Valley Lake Resorts. I enjoyed fishing there and showing off my catch at the end of the day. I enjoyed our conversations, whether in person or over the phone. We would talk about my job as a police officer and all its challenges. We would also talk about everyday life, and I found that those conversation are the ones I will miss most with my dad."

Leah I. James

"My fondest memory of Dad is our time at the table. He always did great impressions of people he did not care too much for. He had funny power struggles with my mom that he would never win. There was never a dull moment. I look forward to being at the table again with my dad and other brothers and sisters in the New Jerusalem."

Caleb E. James

"The Man, The Myth, The Legend.

"First, I would like to say what an honor it is to have called such extraordinary man my father. He has given me a tall order to live up to. He has worn so many hats in his daily life. But I could always tell that fatherhood was the most important to him. Congratulations on your fifteen years of service with St. Louis City Chaplains. I know your efforts will be greatly missed, and just as I've realized there are some big shoes to fill, I'm sure that you have groomed someone that can step in them. I'm glad to see you get the recognition you deserve.

"I love you, Dad, and I appreciate all that you do."

Fond Memories from the Faith Community

"Pastor Emeritus Willie Earl James demonstrated full proof of Matthew 25:35–40, which extended beyond the walls of New Ebenezer Missionary Baptist Church of the Ville: "Whatever you did for one of the least of these brothers and sisters of mine, you did for me." Pastor Emeritus Willie Earl James was committed to the call to serve all mankind."

Reverend Lady Elizabeth R. Smith, True Vine Missionary Baptist Church Ferguson

"Words regarding the Honorable Pastor Emeritus Willie Earl James:
"Unheralded, Unsung, Unsparing."

Bishop Von D. Smith

"Pastor Emeritus Willie Earl James is to be remembered as a pioneer, a great thinker, and a motivator. It was my distinct pleasure to work with, and get to know, this uniquely suited man. Brother Willie Earl James stood tall, spoke directly, and engaged the needy, those marginalized, and those who knew tragedy. Brother Willie Earl James learned to demonstrate love, mercy, and compassion. As a husband, a father, and a man, Willie Earl James gave and received, and he shared his whole life with his special and unique loved ones. Mr. Willie Earl James did his level-best taking responsibility of being an example of a total man. Pastor Emeritus Willie Earl James took to heart the ideas, words, and life of Jesus Christ. Pastor Willie Earl James loved to see growth and change and experience real fellowship. A spiritual giant, champion, and warrior. I am indebted to this remarkable man, Pastor Emeritus Reverend Willie Earl James."

Chelsea Manor Resident Soror Christy Crump

"My fondest memory of Willie would be during his time as president of our subdivision trustees. Whenever I asked him to look into a situation or help to improve our subdivision, he was always prompt and kind to me, and you could tell working with us neighbors brought him joy. I know that you miss him, and we miss seeing him as well."

Bill Heine

"Willie James was always trying to get things done. That is a rare trait and the thing I admired the most about him. I worked with Willie when he was the chairman of our home association for many years. It's the kind of job where you try to build a better community, but it takes a lot of energy to make things happen. I never asked what motivated Willie to have that much energy. But I believe he saw all the problems in the world, and he just wanted to do his part in it and leave it as a better place."

Alex Governal

"I was saying "Hey" to Willie, and he saw that I didn't look good. I explained to him that I was sick, and he offered to cut the grass. I said, "No way, but thank you." And he said, "Boy! Accept your blessings!" And he proceeded to cut the grass. This had a huge impact on me and my outlook on receiving blessings. They can be very hard to receive, but I started realizing the power of selflessness, not just how it makes one look or seem but rather the character and the impact it can have on people.

"The lesson was the real blessing. He also said, "It's awesome!" He shares that story all the time.

"I want to also say thank you, Lord, for people like you and Willie! What a blessing!

"Our best regards,

"Ted and Mary Governal"

Gary and Pat Kleeschulte

We first met Willie James and his family when they moved across the street from us, at first it was just a wave and a "hello" greeting, but over time it became much more. Willie was the kind of person who always had time to stop what he was doing and talk to you. He was very proud of his family and wanting to know how your family was doing also.

He was one of the busiest persons I know. He was a supervisor for Metro, was the Pastor at his church, was a Chaplain for the St. Louis City and County Police and he took on the job as Chairman of the subdivision.

He took all of these jobs very seriously. When he told you he was going to fix or look into a problem you knew it was going to be taken care of.

He was very concerned that our subdivision be kept up to excellent standards, as this is where we lived and he wanted everyone to be proud to have guests come visit.

He will be missed. RIP Willie, you deserve it.

Mary and Gary Anterhaus

"Extraordinary, devoted, and wonderful are a few words to describe Reverend Willie Earl James. He always had a kind gesture or word for us from our very first meeting. There is always a spot in our hearts for such a special person."

Bishop Beulah Brock Brandon Th.D.

"In loving memory of my brother-in-law, Pastor Emeritus Willie Earl James:

"I thank God for that Bi-State bus ride where divine providence, you, and my sister Rev. Dr. Dorothea King-James met. The meeting was necessary for the two of you to complete each other in accordance with God's plans. I must say I was honored to serve as your matron of honor. How rewarding it was for me to see how God, through your union, allowed my sister's joy to be restored and her divine purpose to be revealed as she grew in Christian maturity. It was even more interesting watching the two of you becoming one. Even more amazing was seeing how the both of you migrated through your life challenges. Also, to top that off, seeing the result of all your family members honoring and calling you blessed at your homecoming celebration."

Mr. Jimmie T. King

"Willie was a kind and trustworthy husband to my sister. He was the type of person that would give you the last of what he had. Well, he's no longer with us. I know he is with the Lord.

"We never got to go on our fishing trip together. He told me about the day he went and caught a huge bass. He had the big mouth bass mounted, and he hung it on a wall at home. Well, I never told him that I catch those kinds of fish all the time, but that was Willie's trophy fish. Rest on, my beloved brother-in-law."

Mrs. Patricia Santiago

"My fond memory of my brother-in-law was that he always gave the best, sincerest hugs to me. My pet name for him was "Cousin Willie." I am grateful that he always listened to me. He was always available to listen and give whatever advice was needed."

Valencia Burns-Shireff (Willie's goddaughter, "Cookie")

"My most memories of my godfather, Pastor Emeritus Willie Earl James, is when I was his dialysis technician. He always had a beautiful smile that would light up the room. He was a very humble man. I would sit with him, and we would have such a good time talking about the Lord. I truly miss that with him.

"Another fond memory I had of him was at his birthday party when he danced the night away. To see him enjoy himself like that filled my heart with joy. I think about him all the time, and may he rest in peace."

Cousin James Butler

"Willie Earl James is a man of great listening, of profound understanding, given from
    the Divine, humble in reasonableness that the Lord requests…and his wife honors him by
    biblical standards.

Pastor Charles P. Mason

"Pastor Willie James was a man of high standards. He maintained high standards throughout his entire ministry as an ordained preacher, pastor, evangelist, and excellent teacher of the gospel. Pastor Willie James portrayed a focused serious side, but he also had a great sense of humor! Willie had one of the heartiest laughs I have ever heard!

"Pastor Willie James was a great businessman. His professionalism resonated throughout every business transaction. Willie was a task master. He held himself accountable to finish every task.

"Pastor Willie James was a man of excellence! He had a passion for music. Willie was very skilled and prolific at playing the piano and singing. He sang and played with excitement! I sang with him with the Gospel Harmonizers, a college choir formed at Harris Stowe State College. Willie and I were both tenors.

"Pastor Willie James was extremely proud of his family and all their accomplishments. He was especially proud of his brilliant, loving, devoted wife, Dorothea! He called her his "queen." Willie constantly and joyfully expressed that God had given them a special love for each other.

"Pastor Willie James persevered through several health challenges. With the help of the Lord and his God-sent, loyal, loving, strong, dedicated wife and prayer partner, Willie overcame those challenges many, many times. Willie kept his faith in God throughout his entire life."

Mr. Alex Ray Hogans

"First, I would like to thank Rev. Dr. Dorothea King-James for the blessing that she provided my wife and me by agreeing to be our marriage officiant, and by helping to provide us with what has to be one of the greatest and most powerful moments in our lives, next to the birth of our children!"

"Mr. James was great and successful. I remember when I was a teen and he seemed resolved in my eyes. He knew what he needed to do, and he would get it done; this was the energy that he carried. On the other side, I could see the love he felt for his family from observing times he spent with his grandchildren. He often would help someone who may not be a blood relative at all. This type of demeanor is what I needed to see as a youth, as a young male with dark skin in Saint Louis, Missouri, and I am proud to have witnessed these moments. Now, as a married man and a father of four,

I appreciate what Mr. James had set as an example of what a father could be like firsthand.

"We, the Hogans family, thank you, and we love you!"

Robert Stowers

"As far back as I can remember, there was James McCain ("Pookie"), Willie Earl James, and me. We were in our early teens (twelve to thirteen years of age,) and we stayed on the same street (Aldine). James McCain lived across the street. His father owned a barber shop, which was located on Delmar and Taylor. His dad would let us hang out there, if we didn't get in the way of his customers. We hung out in the backyard of the barber shop. Sometimes, the men would get loud and use foul language.

"James's dad didn't want us to be exposed to that. The best part was that at the end of the day, Pookie's dad would leave us the keys to clean and lock up the barber shop. But before starting, we would go through the shop, find money left in the chairs and food left in the back room from the restaurant next door (Southern Kitchen) and get a free haircut from James McCain.

"There was always a guy named Wine in the backyard. He would use the little money he begged from people to buy liquor. Willie was the one who would always see to it that Wine got some of the food and money left in the shop, even though he knew Wine was going to buy liquor.

"There was never a dull moment on Aldine. Something was always going on. There was the neighborhood troublemaker (Joe Joe) who would always get into a physical altercation with his grandfather, Mr. Doby. Mr. Doby owned neighborhood confectionary, which was right across the street from my house. When Willie was visiting me, we would sit on the porch and wait for the action to start. We knew it was just a matter of time before the fight would begin. Sure enough, it did. It wasn't just a slap or two. It was always a knock-down, drag-out fight. Willie thought that if Joe Joe hung out with us, he would stay out of trouble. That was an experiment gone wrong. Not only did he continue to *stay in* trouble, but Joe Joe started to *get us* in trouble. We decided to let him go his own way.

"Shortly thereafter, Joe Joe was stabbed with an ice pick while trying to rob a paperboy. He later died of internal bleeding.

"Willie always had a passion for music. When his family moved to another part of town, by the old ballpark on Dodier Street, we met Willie Stockard ("Stock") and started a band. The house that Willie stayed in at the time had a third floor. His mother would always tell us to go all the way up to the third floor if we wanted to practice, but hauling all that equipment up to the third floor reduced our practice days to a minimum. Stock played drums, Willie played bass guitar, and I played lead guitar. We thought we were pretty good back then. We played at a lot of good venues and a lot of bad ones, too. It's funny when I think about it. We always seem to remember the bad ones. It seems like the Lord was taking care of us even back then. There were times when we wondered how we got out of those places without being hurt or killed. We shared numerous adventures together, but God had other plans for Willie."

James McCain ("Pookie") and Willie Earl James: The Younger Years in the Hood

Pastor Willie Earl James and I started at the early age of ten years old. We both grew up in the four thousand block of Aldine Avenue in St. Louis, MO. When I first met Willie, he had family that lived directly across the street from my family, and Willie lived on the corner. From the moment I met him, the fun began, and the adventures were many!

Willie and I both had a love of music. At the time, Willie had a guitar, and I had a set of bongos, and we would get together and make as much noise as we could. With all the noise we made, it reached the ears of one of our other neighborhood friends, Robert Stowers. He moved onto the block, and we later discovered he also had a guitar, so we became a mini band of three, which added to our madness! At first, our neighbors would yell for us to stop the noise, but after many evenings of practice after school, our neighbors stopped yelling for us to stop and started to listen to us. Later, our friend Willie Stockard, who had a set of drums, joined us, and then our band was complete. We would perform in talent shows and in nightclubs around town, long before we were old enough to go *into* nightclubs.

During those early years, aside from playing our music, we did as young boys did back in those days: we would all get together and ride our bikes around town, visiting family and friends, as well as take trips to Tandy Park, Wohl's Community Center, and Fairgrounds Park.

Boys being boys, we had the bright idea, one day, to go and get a softball off the roof of a house next to Riddick Elementary, the school we attended as children. Willie, Robert, and I borrowed our neighbor's fifty-foot ladder and walked at least ten long blocks, carrying this ladder all the way to remove what we thought was one softball off the roof of the house. Once we got there with the ladder, we found out there were several balls on the roof of this house! We started our quest to remove all the balls while some of the fellas in the neighborhood started helping themselves to some of the balls. Now the challenge began—making the journey home, not only lugging a fifty-foot ladder, but also carrying all the balls we confiscated off the roof. That was a long, uncomfortable walk back home. We played softball games in the alley and the lots in the hood.

As the years passed, we transitioned from energetic, rambunctious boys with childhood adventures to teenagers. Willie moved from our neighborhood on Aldine to Dodier, which was near Sportsman's Park where the Cardinals and the Big Reds had their baseball and football games. When there were games at the stadium, Willie used his backyard as a parking lot and parked the cars of the game attendees, and I often went to his house to direct the cars down the alley to the parking lot (backyard). We took our hustle from playing in our small band to being parking attendants.

One day, we woke up as young men going in different directions. Willie came to me one day to share with me where God was leading him. Willie expressed his calling to the ministry and his desires to preach the gospel. From the many years we spent together as friends and brothers, I knew his heart and soul was committed to the ministry. My wife, Wanda, and I later joined his church and started our worship with Rev. Willie James at Ebenezer MB Church. Rev. Willie James and I would spend a lot of time talking and discussing political and social issues as well as the crime going on in our communities among the young people and how they were falling away from God. My friend and brother dedicated many years of his life to making a difference in the community to help the lost find their way back to Christ. He devoted his life to improving the lives of everyone he met.

My brother/friend, Rev. Willie Earl James, was a great man. I loved him and will forever cherish the memories we shared.

My fondest memories of Pastor Emeritus Willie Earl James

I met Pastor Willie E. James through Homicide Ministers and Community Alliance (HMCA) in the fall of 2017. He was the ministerial coordinator for Homicide Ministers Community Alliance, who delegated assignments and dispersed information to this organization volunteers. Pastor James network through community resources, businesses, to met the needs of victims' families of a homicide. He was a real team player who has showed compassion for his work and position. I am grateful that, Pastor Willie E. James took me under his proverbial wing and mentored me into this organization. I began to frequently attend their monthly meeting, so that I could continue learning from him and others in this organization.

Pastor James and I would, often have informal lunch meetings; to my surprise he was willing to put the time in and feed me the ministry (spirituality). He taught me some very critical points to be aware of when conducting funerals and memorials. Always know the visual exits!

Sit in the back not the front nor the pulpit; because it's about the family and not about you! Be watchful and remain alert; don't get too comfortable and forget where you are or your purpose. You can leave after your part in the service or wait until it's over; your option.

Pastor James asked me to meet him at a memorial service; one day; and to my surprise it was San Francisco Christian Assembly. I was a member of that church several years , under the leadership of " The Late Bishop Dwight H. McDaniels." I really appreciate Pastor James for dedicating his time to explain not only this ministry; but also the work ethics of this ministry.

Pastor James reminds me so much of my late biological father " Mr. John Lee Carter" in so many ways; they were of both dark complexion, very mild mannered, humble in spirit and true men that believe in their work to better community, family and friends. As our friendship and mutal respect for each other, continue to grow we discovered that we were in union steward (s) on our jobs. I am truly blessed that his nourishing mentoring has continued!

I am appreciative unto God; to have met such an Amazing Man of God! Pastor James has impacted my life and my ministry to the fullest! Pastor Willie E. James and his family has truly blessed me. I will never forget him. Pastor James will forever hold a spot in my heart. If I had, to label our relationship I can only give what God has shown me through him ,simply " An ACT OF KINDNESS" God's blessing to you and your supportive family.

Pastor Leonard Nunn Overseer,
Demonstrate The Love Outreach Ministries

In Tribute to Pastor Willie Earl James

I met Pastor Willie Earl James in 1989 when we both joined a group called ' Clergy and Friends of area III." I had no idea, at the time, that God had placed us in ministry together and our relationship would last for a long time. We went from Clergy and Friends to chaplains of the St. Louis Metropolitan Police Department and St. Louis County Police Department to serving together in a group called Homicide Ministers and Community Alliance (HMCA). In the thirty-two years we served together in ministry, he has always been Pastor James to me because I wanted to give him the respect that title commands.

He deserves it. Pastor James was powerfully subtle. He was a very humble man who was able to teach volumes through his subtlety. Even though he was not officially my pastor, unofficially he was and I was always happy to submit to his leadership. I learned so many things just by watching him.

He lived the life he preached about and without saying a word he also taught how to be committed and dedicated to a calling just by showing his own commitment and dedication.

I quite often think about beginning of our work together. When I joined Clergy and Friends, I was the only female and when they held elections someone decided "let's give secretary to the lady."

In 1989 women still had to fight hard to be accepted in ministry so secretary was a fitting position for a woman. That night Pastor James would treat me as a fellow laborer who was just as able to perform ministry when called on to do so. He assigned things for me to do just like everyone else and commended me for a job well done just like he did everyone else. I didn't realize at the time, but I came to see that Pastor James was pushing me and grooming me. Because of Pastor James I gradually became part of the team. Over thirty-two years I continued to learn from him and appreciated his presence in my life. If I could cite one lesson above all that he taught me I would say that I watched Pastor James in different situations and can always say that no matter what he never gave up and with God's help I am learning to not give up. I thank God for using Pastor James to shape me in ministry and I thank Pastor James for his perpetual willingness to be used by God.

Submitted by *Chaplain Eileen*

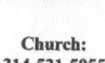 **Greater Faith Missionary Baptist Church**
'City of Love'
4114 West Natural Bridge Avenue
Saint Louis, Missouri 63115
Elder Gina P. Kelley, Pastor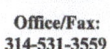

Church:
314-531-5055

Office/Fax:
314-531-3559

"Give me, Savior, a purpose deep,
in joy or sorrow Thy trust to keep
and so thru trouble, care and strife,
glorify Thee in my daily life.
Only on life, 'Twill soon be past;
Only what's done for Christ will last."

October 8, 2021

To Rev. Dorothea James and Family and the New Ebenezer M. B. Church of the Ville:

A Godly life ended. Many hearts are filled with sorrow, but we realize that this homegoing is the greatest experience of PASTOR EMERITUS WILLE E. JAMES' life which was filled with wonderful experiences.

There are three steps to heaven: out of self; into Christ; and then into Glory. PASTOR JAMES took these first two steps in life and lived a beautiful life in Christ. Now he has taken the third step where there is no more weeping, no pain, no sorrow and no disappointments.

PASTOR EMERITUS WILLIE JAMES has fulfilled God's purpose for his life; though we may weep awhile, we should rejoice with him and thank our Heavenly Father for the life he lived among us.

Our prayers are with you. Look to God for strength and peace during this time of challenge.

Prayerfully submitted,

Greater Faith Missionary Baptist Church "City of Love"
Elder Gina P. Kelley, Pastor

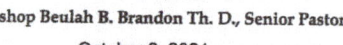

Shiloh Praise & Worship Center of Empowerment Shiloh-PWCOE

8319 Halls Ferry Road

Baden, MO 63147-2323

314-643-5369

Bishop Beulah B. Brandon Th. D., Senior Pastor

October 8, 2021,

The Lord gave and the has taken away;
may the name of the Lord be praised. Job 1:21

To the James family and New Ebenezer Missionary Baptist Church family, relatives, and friends; we offer our heartfelt sympathy in this great loss to you, but to Heaven a gain. God has granted Willie Earl James an upgrade from homeward bound to a Heavenly home.

Remember that he lived intentionally to make an impact in this earth realm with the gifts and talents that God graced him with (To name a few: Pastor, Teacher, Husband, father, and Police Chaplain). He gracefully offered his gifts as a servant submitted and committed to God first, thus allowing him to humbly submit to earthly leadership. He was always willing to help and encourage others through their trauma whenever the need arose for his service.

God has now given him rest from his **laboring as a disciple for Him on earth to eternal rest in heaven with Him**. So, weep as it is part of the cleansing process associated with grief. Don't stay there, move as directed by the word of God in

2 Corinthians 1:3-4:
   Praise be to our God and Father of our Lord Jesus Christ,
   the Father of compassion and the God of all comfort,
   who comforts us in all our troubles,
   so that we can comfort those in any trouble with the comfort
   we ourselves have received from God.

Thanks be to God for his moving out of his old house to a new home in Glory. If you need us, we are only a phone call away.

Humbly submitted by

Trinity Full Gospel/Shiloh Praise & Worship Center International
Bishop Beulah B Brandon TH. D, Senior Pastor

"I will bless the Lord at all times: His praise shall continually be in my mouth. My soul shall me her boast in the Lord: the humble shall hear thereof, and be glad. O magnify the Lord with me, and let us exalt His name together." Psalm 34:1-3

Dearest Sister-in Christ, the Reverend Dr. Dorothea King-James,

The Lord in Isaiah 6 asks "whom shall I send? And who will go for us?" **Reverend WILLIE EARL JAMES** answered, "Here am I, send me"> He answered the unction in Isaiah 6:8b to go into the highways and the hedges and compel men/women and boys/girls to accept Jesus as their saviour.

His gentle compassionate manner was a beacon within the community and the city of St. Louis at large. **REV. WILLIE JAMES** let it be known that you, my sister, were the love of his life and his true partner...his 1st Lady! You, likewise, exemplified the sincere characteristics of a helpmeet (Genesis 1) or complimentary companion.

It is such a blessing that you both honored every aspects of your vows: in sickness and in health; through life's challenges and as co-laborers for the Master.

Great news: I can attest the LOVE lives beyond the grave! Even though you will forever miss his shell, the Lord's Promises will sustain you and the entire family. Your memories will be the soothing balm as you individually grieve this separation. Know that the prayerful intercessory support of your Big Sister/Prayer Partner is a virtual hug whenever you need it.

Lovingly,

Florida Cowley
Phil. 1:3

ST. LOUIS AIRPORT INTERFAITH CHAPLAINCY, INC.
LAMBERT – ST. LOUIS INTERNATIONAL AIRPORT
P.O. BOX 10295, Lambert Station
St. Louis, MO 63145-0295

Chapel/Office Located at Exit 14, Main Terminal
(Baggage Carousel/Concourse Level)
Telephone (314) 427-8787

October 8, 2021

2 Timothy 4:6-8 – For I am now ready to be offered, and the time of my departure is at hand. I have fought a good fight; I have finished my course, I have kept the faith: Henceforth there is laid up for me a crown of righteousness, which the Lord, the righteous judge, shall give me at that day: and not to me only, but unto all them also that love his appearing.

To: The Family of Rev Willie James

We express our deepest sympathy to your family in the passing of loved one, Rev Willie James, and are in prayer with you. We know that his presence will be missed, but we encourage you to look to God and be assured that the God who gives life physically and spiritually has already taken him into His divine arms and welcomed him into His heavenly home.

May the Lord sustain you in the coming days and shower you with grace and peace.

Humbly and Prayerfully Submitted By,

Reverend Rodrick Burton
President
St. Louis Airport Interfaith Chaplaincy

Sumner High School

4248 West Cottage
St. Louis, Mo 63113
October 8, 2022

> "I will trust in the Lord with all my heart and lean not to thine own understanding but in all thy ways acknowledge Him, and he shall direct thy paths" (Proverbs 3:5–6).

The 1968 Class of Sumner High School expresses its heartfelt sympathy to the entire James family in the transition of your dearly beloved, Pastor Emeritus Willie Earl James. God, in His infinite power, has completed Pastor Emeritus Willie Earl James's abode for eternity. Today, we celebrate the life of a treasure link removed from the James family, the 1968 Sumner High School Class, and the New Ebenezer Missionary Baptist Church, where our classmate served as Pastor. Pastor Emeritus Willie Earl James was truly loved by his dear wife of forty-two years, the Reverend Dr. Dorothea King-James; his family; his Sumner Alumni; and his church family.

Pastor Emeritus Willie Earl James expressed musical appreciation during his tenure at Sumner High School and at his church. Pastor Emeritus Willie Earl James was a friend to many, who greeted you with a gentle smile and kind spirit. His memory will live forever in the minds and hearts of his family and those he met and loved. Thank God for time shared and bonded relationships on his journey here. We encourage you to trust in the Lord and cast all your cares on Him. Let not your heart be troubled; reflect on the good times for strength in the coming days, months, and years. Keep the faith and allow the comfort of the Holy Spirit to sustain you. We pray God's unconditional love, compassion, and promises will give you peace in the matchless name of Jesus. God bless you all and stay safe.

Prayerfully submitted,
The 1968 Class of Sumner High School
Herman Jones, President

Salute To My Father

A Salute to My Father
Pastor Willie Earl James

The love of my Father will always be one of the most potent moral forces in my life. My dad was my real-life superhero. I talked to my dad nearly every day, and I miss him immensely.

I remember, when I was a child, my dad would say, "Die empty. Don't allow fear or others' opinions of you distract you from doing what God has called you to do and to move when God deems so. Don't linger when people let you down, for all have fallen short of the glory of God. Don't lay up your treasures on Earth and material things, for material things will surely wither away."

My father lived his life with the end in mind. He laid up his treasures in heaven. He not only preached but taught the gospel. My dad will always be my favorite preacher. He gathered as many souls as he could for Christ, and I physically witnessed my dad save lives, minister to those in need, and give sound advice in even the most difficult situations. I am forever grateful to have witnessed my dad fulfilling his calling. He was a true definition of servant leader, serving his employer as a transit service manager, his church as a pastor, and community as a police chaplain.

My father loved with the end in mind. He loved my mother. Those two…what a wonderful example of what love is and truly can be.

God blessed them with forty-two beautiful years of matrimony together. I loved watching their interactions with each other; they were hilarious when they got worked-up. Their example of love and marriage showed me that anything in life worth having takes work, patience, forgiveness, consistency, empathy, laughter, and consideration. Their love was truly beautiful, and I am grateful to have witnessed this for over thirty-five years. My dad not only spoke of his love and dedication to my mother and their children but showed it consistently through his actions. Even until his last breath.

I love you, Dad, and I am forever grateful for your love, for your example, and your legendary legacy.

Respectfully submitted,
Your BG

This was the last constructed sermon written by Pastor Emeritus Willie Earl James.

"It's All Good"

My friends, I think I can't go without saying that March 2020 up to this present time have been some difficult months for many of us. As a matter of fact, to say that the past months have been challenging is probably an understatement. These have been months when we had to make constant adjustments in the midst of uncertainties, months where questions have outweighed answers. Months that we have never sailed through before. Seeing businesses shut down while others go out of business, never to open again. We had to witness children having to stay at home from school and struggle with online education in ways that help our children, while sitting in front of a computer screen at home. We've had to deal with an inescapable presence of the valley of the shadow of death. COVID-19 has claimed over 700,000 lives in the state of Florida alone. These certainly have been some difficult months. As we enter a new year, we come into it almost asking the same question that Gideon asked: "If God is with us, why is this happening to us?" Beloved, none of us are immune from that question; life can put you in such a bind because you are dealing with so many uncertainties, struggles, and sufferings. If you, like Gideon, would say, "If God is with us, why is all this happening to us?" in the midst of these uncertain days and struggles of our season we find ourselves navigating through, I come to share with you a word from the Lord to let you know that God is still on the throne. I would ask you to turn to your Bible with me to a passage of scripture in it, but I am afraid you won't need your Bible for this verse. If you have been raised in church for any amount of time, my gut feeling is that you know this scripture:

"Weeping may endure for a night, but joy comes in the morning."
This verse can be compared to "No weapon form against me shall prosper."
"They that wait on the Lord shall renew their strength."

In the book of Romans 8:28, you will find these words of Paul as he declares this (New International Bible): "And we know that in all things, God works for the good of those who have been called according to his purpose." Please look at the person next to you and tell them these words: "It's all good." My friends, Romans 8:28 is a verse that can hold you together when it seems like life is trying to pull you in another direction.

Romans 8:28 is what you remind yourself of when bad news catches you off-guard.

Romans 8:28 is what you speak over your life when you find out that your friends are fake and your enemies are real.

Romans 8:28 is what you tell yourself when you wake up in the morning, and you look at yourself in the mirror and know it's about to be a rough day.

Romans 8:28 is what you quote when it seems like everything in your life is going from bad to worst.

Romans 8:28 is what you meditate on when you are anxious or uncertain, and you don't know how things are going to work out.

Romans 8:28. That's what you quote when you look at or hear the news of the day as it relates to the happenings in our world today.

Yet, you remind yourself of this:

"We know that in all things, God works for the good of those who love Him, who have been called according to his purpose."

As we look at this text, who are the "we?" The answer is found at the end of the verse. "Those who love God and been called according to his purpose."

How do you know I know?
I've seen God make a way out of no way.
I've seen God answer prayer.
I've seen God go over and beyond what I asked Him to do.
I've seen God turn a life around.
I've seen someone that was sick enough to die, but well enough to live.
I've seen God open a door that no one could close.
I've seen God turn weeping into joy.
I've seen God do great things in my life.
What have you seen God do?

Pastor Emeritus Willie Earl James

Thirty-Eighth Church Anniversary Speech

Introduction for
38th Church Annual Celebration
for
New Ebenezer Missionary Baptist Church of the Ville

We honor God because He is God! It states in Proverbs 18:22 that "He who finds a wife finds a good thing and obtains favor of the Lord." I am my husband's "good thing," and I stand today to formally introduce Pastor Emeritus Willie Earl James. "Some people succeed by what they know, some by what they do, and a few, by what they are." My husband has succeeded for all those reasons. Just recently, he completed specialized training through the United States Homeland Security, Federal Law Enforcement, and earned a new title as Adjunct Instructor. He has proven to be a man of tact, integrity, warmth, and wisdom. It's my esteemed honor that I present to our church family my "Best Friend," Pastor Emeritus Willie Earl James.

APPENDIX

Appendix Image One:
ORIGINAL BUS TRANSFER FROM OUR INITIAL MEETING

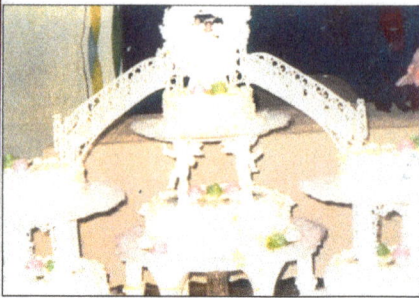

Appendix Image Two:
OUR WEDDING CEREMONY

Appendix Image Three:
FIRST YEAR OF MARRIAGE

Appendix Image Four:
THIRTY-SEVEN REASONS FOR OUR LOVE

Appendix Image Five:
WE JUMPED THIS BROOM ON OUR WEDDING DAY

Appendix Image Six:
HUSBAND & WIFE

Appendix Image Seven:
**PASTOR EMERTIUS WILLIE EARL JAMES &
MINISTER MELVIN CLARK**

To You From Me

Reverend Willie James

I CRAVE YOUR HONESTY ON THE DAY OF LOVE,

LOVE YOU WHOLEHEARTEDLY MY SWEET DOVE.

OUT OF THE BLUE YOU SHOUT FROM THE SKY,

VIVIDLY, BEAUTIFULLY STUNNING MY EYE.

EVER ADORING YOU IS WHAT I DO BEST,

YOUR SMILE, YOUR FACE AND ALL THE REST.

ON DAYS LIKE THESE I TRULY BELIEVE,

U AND I ARE MEANT TO BE.

Appendix Image Eight:
TO YOU FROM ME- HUSBAND'S ORIGINAL POEM

LOVE IS A TREASURED KEEPSAKE

By Dr. Dorothea King-James

Love is a treasured keepsake
You never want to lose it
When you discover this treasure you'll
always strive to protect it
Always desiring to caress it and hold it
Deep within your arms!

This treasure makes you smile in the midst
of your finite pain,
It will evoke laughter when your body is
strained,
Love is a treasure keepsake,
You never want to abuse it
Because this treasure is far to precious
To lose it!

Written March 8, 2010 @
Sumner High School

Appendix Image Nine:
LOVE IS A TREASURED KEEPSAKE- WIFE'S ORIGINAL POEM

Appendix Image Ten:
**NEW EBENEZER MISSIONARY BAPTIST CHURCH OF THE VILLE
OUR PLACE OF WORSHIP FOR FORTY-THREE YEARS**

Appendix Image Eleven:
PASTOR EMERITUS WILLIE EARL JAMES- BIBLE STUDY

Appendix Image Twelve:
HUSBAND'S TROPHY FISH

Appendix Image Thirteen:
THE MAN, THE MYTH, THE LEGEND

Appendix Image Fourteen:
**OUR 35ᵀᴴ ANNIVERSARY
INITIAL CAKE "W" AND "D"**

Appendix Image Fifteen:
**CELEBRANTS DOROTHEA AND WILLIE
SEATED AT TABLE OF HONOR**

Appendix Image Sixteen:
SEALING OUR JOY WITH A KISS

Appendix Image Seventeen:
CELEBRANTS HOLDING KNIFE BEFORE CUTTING THE CAKE

Appendix Image Eighteen:
WE ARE ACTUALLY CUTTING OUR CAKE

Appendix Image Nineteen:
WIFE PLACING CAKE INTO WILLIE'S MOUTH

Appendix Image Twenty:
HUSBAND PLACING CAKE INTO DOROTHEA'S MOUTH

Appendix Image Twenty-One:
**HUSBAND AND WIFE HOLDING HANDS
IN FRONT OF OUR HOME**

Appendix Image Twenty-Two:
HUSBAND DEPOSIT A KISS ON WIFE FACE- A MOMENT OF INTIMACY

Works Cited

The Bible. The Spurgeon Study Bible. Christian Standard Bible. Holman Bible Publishers, 2017.

The Holy Bible. King James Version, Reference Edition, Publishers, November, 2010.

The Bible. New King James Version, "A Woman After God's Own Heart, "Kregel Publications 2018.

New International Bible. Quest Study Bible Revised, Zondervan 1994 2003.

United States Marine Corp., a USMC recruiting slogan, Anonymous.

Th "L" Theory: "Live". "Laugh." "Love." Anonymous.

"God is Our Encouragement," Tribute poem, Anonymous.

Eiland, F.J. and Dean, Emmet S. The New National Baptist Hymnal. "Keep Me Everyday." Triad Publishing, 2018.

James, Willie E., original poem, " From Me to You," 2008.

James, Dorothea King, original poem, "Love is A Treasured Keepsake," May 8, 2010.

James, Dorothea King, " From Tribulations To Triumphs, " 2009

ABOUT THE AUTHOR

The Reverend Doctor Dorothea Louise King-James is the beloved wife of forty-two years to Reverend Willie Earl James, Pastor Emeritus of New Ebenezer Missionary Baptist Church of the

Ville. She is the magnificent mother of four daughters and three sons. She is a retired educator who served Saint Louis Public Schools for thirty-six years. She served the district as a resource specialist who developed curriculum to meet the needs of mentally challenged youth. The author enjoys quiet walks and communing with God daily. It is in God that she moves and has her total being.

Dorothea endeavors to share frequent challenges and tests in her relationship with God Jehovah and others. As depicted in the manuscript, within her family circle came births, marriages, illnesses, and death.

Waves of Faith depicts the author's personal journey shared through hardships of faith, struggles, and victory obtained, because, for better or worse, every human being is born into a family that shapes who and what he or she becomes. The author wishes to reveal how God Jehovah allows us a special opportunity to reflect upon our past positive and negative life challenges to visualize just how good the Lord has been.

The Lord has seen Dorothea through joblessness, poverty, homelessness, and separations.

Through her story, she hopes readers will see that new love can be developed and experienced through the nurturing of the Christian family. The author has truly persevered through much and wishes to leave this, her story, as a legacy for her children, their children, and their children's children, letting them know that if they continue to put their total trust and confidence in Almighty God, He will bring them out of any future adversities that may abruptly push them out of their comfort zones.

Dorothea shouts that the Lord sits high and looks low and has brought her through her waves of faith, because she personally found new life in Him. She thanks and praises God's name forever for giving more than enough victory through her unforeseen storms.

www.ingramcontent.com/pod-product-compliance
Lightning Source LLC
LaVergne TN
LVHW051040070526
838201LV00067B/4879